I WANT TO KNOW ABOUT......©.
Volume 1
Section A

ANIMAL BABIES

By Illa Podendorf

Laboratory School
University of Chicago

A fascinating story of baby animals, told by a teacher of science for children just beginning to feel some measure of independence from adult care. It is the story of many baby animals from goslings to elephants that must be cared for while they are young.

There is the baby bat clinging to its mother's fur while she sails through the air and then, when it is big enough, left hanging upside down on a limb while she goes to hunt for food. There are baby opossums staying snug in their mother's pouch for ten weeks before they climb out to ride on her back.

There is the wonder of the baby turtles, alligators, tr ut that take care of themselves from the first and may never see their parents.

ANIMAL BABIES

By Illa Podendorf

Illustrations by Pauline Adams

 CHILDRENS PRESS, CHICAGO

GROLIER ENTERPRISES, CANADA

CONTENTS

Some animal babies must be
  cared for by grown-up animals . . . 6

Some animal babies take care
  of themselves 30

Some animal babies change a
  great deal as they grow up 33

All animal babies come from
  big animals like themselves 35

SOME ANIMAL BABIES MUST BE CARED FOR BY GROWN-UP ANIMALS

Many kinds of young animals are not able to take care of themselves. Most of them are taken care of by their mothers.

Baby lambs cannot take care of themselves. Sometimes the mothers need help. Would you like to help care for a baby lamb?

A baby bat clings to its
mother's fur as she sails
through the air.

When the baby is big enough,
the mother hangs it upside down.
She leaves it while she goes
to hunt food for herself.

Lion cubs depend on both
their fathers and their mothers
for food and protection.

A mother deer hides her fawn
among tall plants. This helps
protect it from its enemies.

Baby opossums are very tiny.
They have no hair and cannot see.

Baby opossums live in their
mother's pouch. When they are
about eight weeks old, they come
out and ride on her back. Now
they have hair. See how they
hold on.

When kittens are very young, they are not fluffy. They cannot see and they cannot walk. Kittens change a great deal while they are young.

A colt looks much like a grown-up
horse. Its legs are wobbly, but a
colt can walk when it is only a few
hours old.

Very young camels can walk,
too, but their legs are not
strong enough for long trips.

When skunks are a few weeks
old, they hunt food with their
mother.

They walk behind each other.

A baby hippopotamus lives
in water with its mother. It
rides on her back when she
swims in deep water.

Little rabbits grow up in a few
weeks. Then they take care of
themselves. Their mother may have
another family to care for by that
time. A mother rabbit may raise
three families in one summer.

Most foxes have birthdays in April. Baby foxes live with their father and mother in a den. They come out when they are about four weeks old. They are fully grown by September.

Most beavers have birthdays in
May. When the young are four weeks
old, they begin eating plant food
as their parents do. In about two
years, they are fully grown.

Most baby bears have birthdays in the winter. They stay in their mother's den where they sleep and drink milk.

The mother brings them out when they are a few months old. Then they hunt for other food.

When bears are about two
years old, they are able to
look after themselves.

See the baby elephant's woolly coat.
Grown-up elephants do not have woolly
coats. Elephants are not fully grown
until they are about twenty years old.

Our baby brothers and sisters
depend on our mothers to feed
them, dress them, carry them,
and keep them comfortable.

Most of us depend on our parents until we are grown. They give us food, clothing, and a home.

They teach us many things and send us to school. We are not really adults until we are about eighteen years old.

The babies you have been reading about depend on milk for food when they are very young.

Their mothers' bodies make milk out of some of the food they eat. The milk is stored in milk glands. The babies nurse the milk from the milk glands.

Some kinds of babies do not
drink milk. Their fathers and
mothers hunt food for them.

The picture shows you the
kind of food baby robins eat.
Tiny robins have almost no
feathers. They get feathers when
they are about eleven days old.

Baby geese are called goslings.
Goslings have down on their bodies
when they are hatched. They get
feathers later.

When they are tiny, their mothers
take them for their first swim.

A mother bobwhite and her babies run about. They find food here and there.

Robins, geese, and bobwhites are alike in a special way. They all get feathers. Can you think of another way? Did you think of wings? Did you think of beaks?

ALLIGATORS

CROCODILES

SOME ANIMAL BABIES
TAKE CARE OF THEMSELVES

Baby alligators and crocodiles
hunt their own food. They will
probably never see their fathers
or mothers.

30

Baby turtles hunt for food
soon after they are hatched.
They will probably never know
their father or mother.

Baby grasshoppers find food
for themselves.

Baby trout hunt their own food.

SOME ANIMAL BABIES CHANGE A GREAT
DEAL AS THEY GROW UP

A young frog does not look much
like a frog. It is a tadpole.

A tadpole loses its tail and gets
legs as it grows up. It also loses
its gills and gets lungs. Then it
is a frog.

A very young Luna moth
does not look much like a grown-up
moth. It is a caterpillar. It will
spin a cocoon about itself and change
into a grown-up Luna moth.

ALL ANIMAL BABIES COME FROM BIG ANIMALS LIKE THEMSELVES

Some animals lay eggs. Each egg has an egg cell inside it. The egg cell may grow into an animal baby.

Ostrich eggs are about as big as twelve chicken eggs. A baby ostrich is about as big as a mother hen.

A hummingbird's egg is no bigger than a pea. Think about how small the baby must be.

Mice do not lay eggs. Mother mice have egg cells inside of their bodies. The egg cells may grow into baby mice. Mice are not much bigger than jelly beans when they are born.

Whales do not lay eggs. They, too, have egg cells inside their bodies. A baby whale may be as big as an elephant.

Cardinals lay eggs. The eggs have egg cells inside of them.

An egg cell may grow into a baby animal if it is kept at the right temperature for the right number of days. What is happening in the picture?

Mother cardinals and meadowlarks lay eggs and cover them with their warm bodies.

Eggs must be protected from their enemies, too. A mother meadowlark hides her nest where it cannot be easily seen.

HEN'S EGG
at 21 days

cell food air

BIRD'S EGG

In a bird's egg is the tiny egg
cell which grows into the baby bird.
There is also food and a space filled
with air.

The baby bird will need food
and oxygen as it grows.

A robin must sit on her
nest fourteen days before
the eggs will hatch.
A mother hen must sit
on her nest twenty-one days
before the eggs will hatch.

A mother duck must sit on her nest twenty-eight days before the eggs will hatch.

When a baby bird is ready to hatch, it breaks the shell of the egg and comes out. It breaks the shell with a sharp point on the end of its beak.

The eggs of other kinds of animals are kept warm by the sun.

ALLIGATOR EGGS
(about 3¼ inches or
8 centimeters long)

BLACK SNAKE EGGS
(about 2 inches or
5 centimeters long)

TURTLE EGGS
(about 1 inch or
2½ centimeters long)

Not all animal babies are hatched. Many animal babies are born.

A baby that is born comes from its mother's body. It grows from a tiny egg cell.

The baby is carried inside the mother's body while it grows big enough to be born. Before it is born, the baby gets its food from the food its mother eats. It gets oxygen from the air its mother breathes.

Some animals have one baby at a time. Look again at pages 15 and 17. Other animals have more than one baby at a time. Look at pages 12 and 26. How many babies were there?

It takes fifteen days for baby hamsters to be big enough to be born.

It takes nine weeks for baby puppies to be big enough to be born.

It takes nine months for our baby brothers and sisters to be big enough to be born. For a baby elephant, it takes twenty-two months—almost two years.

All babies that are born drink milk during the first part of their lives. Baby animals that are hatched eat many other kinds of food.

SOUNDS WE HEAR

By Illa Podendorf

Science on primary level, encouraging new sensitiveness to sounds—how they are made and how they are heard.

From the human ear and other animal ears that are similar, the author goes to grasshoppers whose ears are hidden under their wings, and crickets with ears on their legs and other animals with strange and interesting ways of hearing.

Sounds that animals make have meaning, in fact, there is meaningful sound all around us. Better understanding of it brings new receptiveness to the wonders of the world we live in.

SOUNDS

we hear

by ILLA PODENDORF

illustrated by Chauncey Maltman

CHILDRENS PRESS, CHICAGO

GROLIER ENTERPRISES, CANADA

TABLE OF

We Hear Sounds 6

Sounds Are Caused
by Vibrations 8

We Hear With Our Ears . . 11

Other Animals Hear Sounds 13

CONTENTS

We Make Sounds 20

Other Animals Make Sounds 23

Some Sounds Are Pleasant . 33

Many Sounds Have Meaning 36

WE HEAR SOUNDS

Hearing is one way to observe what is happening around us. We may hear something blowing in the wind when we do not feel it.

We may hear a puppy barking when we do not see it.

We may hear a telephone ringing.
We may hear a baby laughing.
Hearing is a very important way to learn what is going on around us.
It is one way to observe.

SOUNDS ARE CAUSED BY VIBRATIONS

All sounds are caused by something moving back and forth very fast.

When something moves back and forth very fast we say it VIBRATES.

Vibrations are not easy to see.

A vibration causes sound waves in the air.

When wind blows leaves they make a sound.

Sometimes we can observe the leaves moving in three ways. We can hear them, see them and feel them.

Although we cannot see sound waves,
sometimes we can see and feel
what causes them.

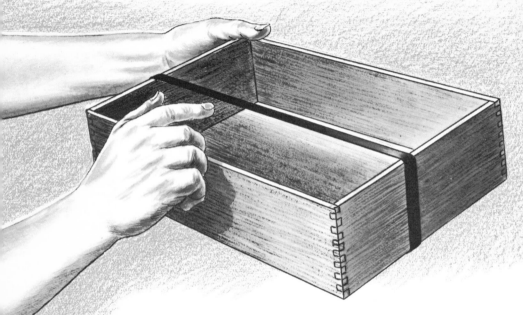

We can stretch a rubber band across
a box and pick it with a thumb or
finger. We cannot see the sound waves
between it and us, but we can hear
the sound it makes. We can see and
feel the vibrations too.

WE HEAR WITH OUR EARS

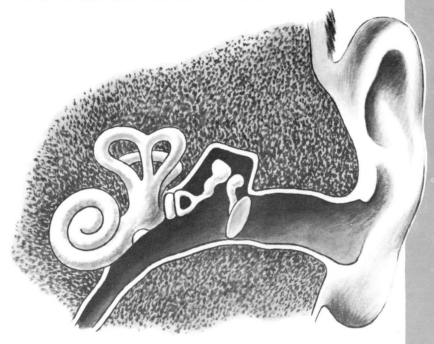

We have an ear drum in each ear which starts to vibrate when sound waves hit it. The ear drum causes three little bones to vibrate.

The nerves in our ears pick up the vibration and carry the messages to the brain. Then we hear.

Is this girl helping her ears to pick up sound waves? Do as she is doing.

We must take good care of our ears. We should never put anything into them, or poke at them with anything which has a sharp point. It might break the ear drum.

OTHER ANIMALS HEAR SOUNDS

Many other animals hear much
the same way as we do.

Dogs are able to hear sounds
that we cannot hear. They can
hear whistles that are made for
calling them. We cannot hear the sounds
the whistles make when we use them.

A rabbit's long ears are useful
to help catch sound waves. A rabbit
needs to hear sounds of danger.

A long-eared owl gets its name
because of the feathers that stand
up like ears. These tall feathers
are not ears. The ears are hidden
under the feathers on each side
of its head.

A robin has one ear on each side
of its head. Its ears are hidden
under its feathers, too.

Alligators live in water. Folds of heavy skin keep the water out of their ears.

The round pieces of thick skin on each side of a frog's head are its ears. Water cannot get into its ears. Can you see the ear back of the eye in the picture?

A grasshopper's ears are well protected. They are on the sides of its body under its wings. They are small and round.

A cricket's ears are on its front legs. They look like small white spots.

WE MAKE SOUNDS

When we talk or sing the vocal cords in our throats vibrate and make sound waves.

Place your hand against your throat and hum a little tune. You can feel the vibration.

When we whistle we cause our lips to vibrate and make sound waves in the air.

When we play music we cause
something to vibrate.

The strings on a violin vibrate.

We can make footsteps.
We can ring a bell.
We can clap our hands.
We can knock on a door.
Tap on many different objects
and listen to the different sounds.

OTHER ANIMALS MAKE SOUNDS

Some birds sing beautiful songs.
Vocal cords in their throats
vibrate and make the sounds.

23

CHICK-A-DEE

WHIP-POOR-WILL

BOB-WHITE

Some kinds of birds have been given their names because of the sounds they make.

Bats make some sounds that we cannot hear. Only bats can hear them.

Wolves and coyotes howl.

Cattle bawl.

Sheep bleat.

Lions and tigers roar.

Seals bark.

Elephants trumpet.

Elk bugle.

Grizzly bears
growl and
roar.

Bees, flies and some other kinds
of insects make buzzing sounds
with their wings as they fly.

Termites and some kinds of beetles make a tapping sound. They make the sound by bumping their heads against the wood of their nests.

A cricket has a file and a
scraper on each front wing cover.
　　He makes a chirp by rubbing a
file of one wing against the
scraper of the other wing.
　　A cricket is sometimes called
an insect musician.

SOME SOUNDS ARE PLEASANT

Some of the more pleasant sounds
we call music.

Some sounds are loud and
unpleasant. We call them noise.

A door banging is an unpleasant
sound.

MANY SOUNDS HAVE MEANING

When our baby brothers and sisters
learn to talk they are really
learning to make sounds that
have meaning.

The sound of a car horn has
meaning. It warns us that a car
is near, and that we should watch
where we are going.

A train whistle warns us to stay
off the track. A train whistle
may mean many other things, too.

A dog's growl warns us that he
is not friendly, or that there is
danger if we come closer.

A rattlesnake's rattle is a warning
that we should stay away.

A wolf's howl
calls other wolves
to join him
in a hunt.

Pigs sometimes squeal when they
see the farmer coming with food.

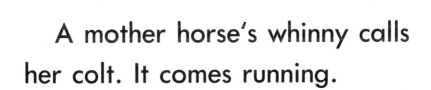

A mother horse's whinny calls
her colt. It comes running.

Beavers warn other beavers of
danger by slapping the water with
their tails.

An alligator's bellow attracts a mate.
The sound is so loud sometimes
that people think it is thunder.

Toads make a pleasant trilling
sound. It is almost as though they
are showing off for their mates.

Some birds act as though they sing for their mates.

But a ruffed grouse drums. He beats the air with his wings which makes the sound.

Some animals make several different kinds of sounds that appear to have meaning.

A hen often cackles when she has laid an egg.

She clucks and her baby chicks come for food.

45

A kitten purrs when it appears
to be happy.

It mews when it is hungry.

It spits when it is
frightened.

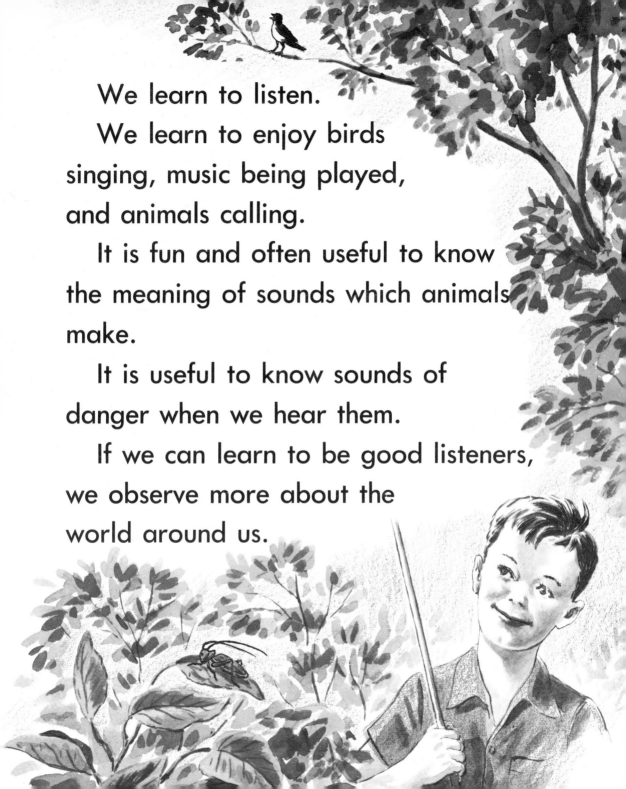

We learn to listen.

We learn to enjoy birds singing, music being played, and animals calling.

It is fun and often useful to know the meaning of sounds which animals make.

It is useful to know sounds of danger when we hear them.

If we can learn to be good listeners, we observe more about the world around us.

MOON SUN AND STARS

By John Lewellen

John Lewellen tells beginning readers about the Moon, Sun and Stars in simple text enlivened with Lois Fisher's amusing drawings.

He tells what the moon is made of and how it moves around the earth. He shows the relationship of the spinning earth to the moon, the sun, and other stars.

With respect for their intelligence and curiosity, he offers some big ideas to little people.

John Lewellen has built a reputation for making difficult subjects interesting and understandable. His recent, popular book on astronomy for older children is YOU AND SPACE NEIGHBORS.

MOON
SUN
and
STARS

By John Lewellen

Pictures by Lois Fisher

 CHILDRENS PRESS, CHICAGO

GROLIER ENTERPRISES, CANADA

TABLE OF

The moon is smaller
than a star................8

The moon moves
around the earth.......12

The moon is
made of rock...........14

The moon is
like a mirror............18

The earth is like
a mirror, too...........22

CONTENTS

The sun is a star.......24

The stars we see
are burning..........26

The earth is turning....30

The earth goes
around the sun........38

"Shooting stars"
are not stars..........43

When you look at the sky
at night, something plays
a trick on you.
The moon looks bigger
than the stars.

The moon is much smaller than the stars and the sun.
It is much smaller than the earth.

THE
LITTLE ONE
IS THE
MOON

EARTH

But the moon is much
    closer to us than any
    star.
It is closer than the sun.
That is why it looks so big.
Hold a penny close to
    your eye.
It looks big.
Look at it across the room.
It looks small.

ONE CENT

The moon moves around
the earth. It makes one
trip in about four weeks.
We never see the other
side of the moon.
Television cameras on space-
crafts have photographed
the other side of the moon.

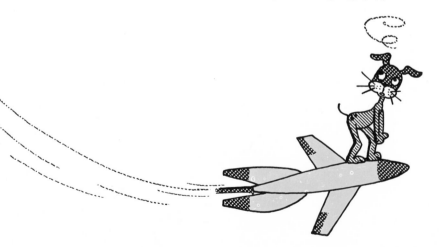

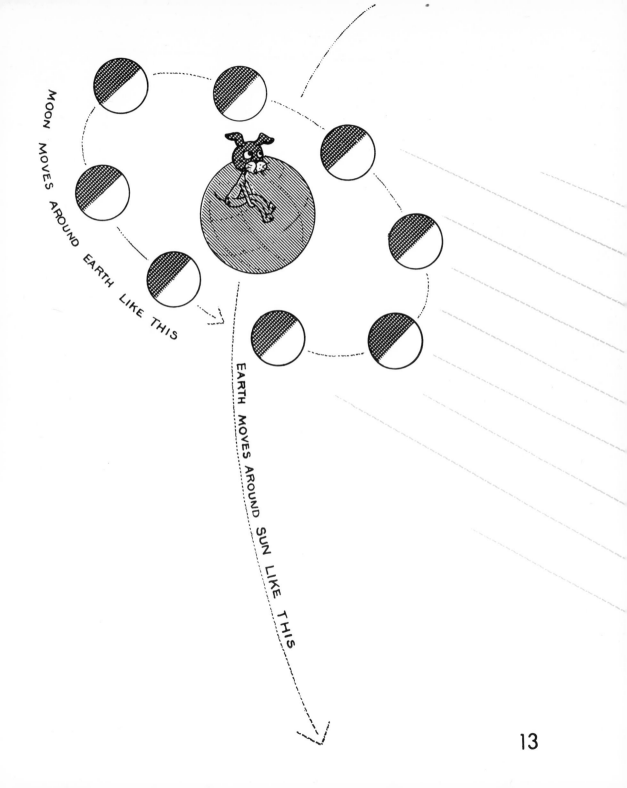

MOON MOVES AROUND EARTH LIKE THIS

EARTH MOVES AROUND SUN LIKE THIS

13

The moon looks flat to us.
But it is a round ball, like
the earth.
The moon is not made of
green cheese.
It is made of rock.
People once thought there
was a "man in the moon"
What looks like "a man in
the moon" are
mountains
and holes
and flat rocks.

14

Also, the moon would be
too hot or too cold.
Days and nights on the
moon are two weeks
long.
Our days are not so hot
as days on the moon.
If they were, our rivers
and lakes would boil.
Our nights are not so cold
as nights on the moon.
If they were, none of our
plants and animals
could live.

People once
thought the
moon had fires
on it.
They thought the
fires made it
bright.
Now we know the
moon is like a
mirror.
It gets its light from
the sun.

We see only that
part of the moon
lighted by the
sun.
The rest of the
moon is there,
but most of the
time it is too
dark to be seen.
That is why the
moon seems to
change its shape
during the month.

You can see how this
works with a ball.
Let the ball be the moon.
Let your head be the earth.
Let the light be the sun.
Turn around with the ball.

You will see the shapes of
the moon.
The ball also shows why
we see only one side of
the moon.
As you turned with the
ball, you saw the same
side of the ball all the
way around.
The moon turns around
once itself while going
around the earth. The
ball did the same thing.
We see only one side.

The earth shines,
too. The earth is
like a mirror, too.

If you were on the moon,
the earth would look
bright when the sun was
shining on it.
It would look much like
the moon, but bigger.

The light of the moon
comes from the sun.
Our daylight comes from
the sun.
What is the sun?
The sun is a star. The stars
we can see have their
own light.
There are many big stars
we can not see. Their
light has burned out.
Others are still bright,
but they are so far

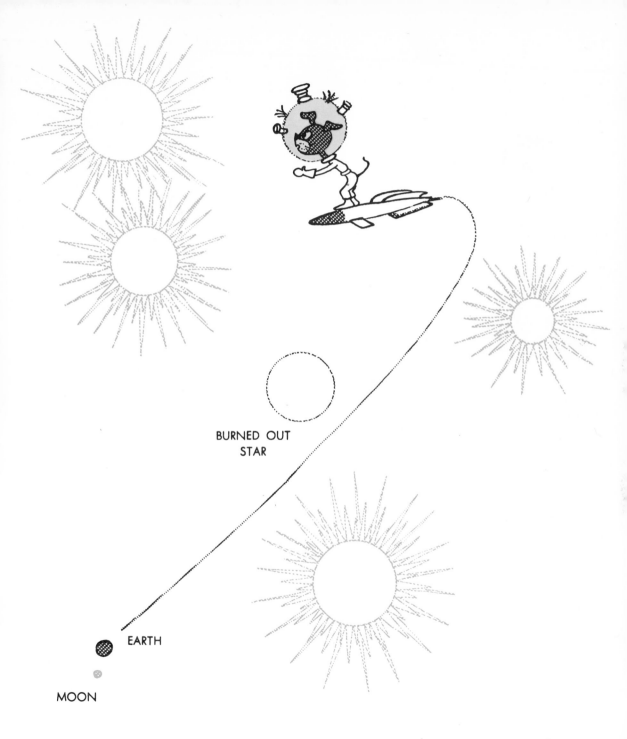

BURNED OUT
STAR

EARTH

MOON

away we can not see
them.

The sun looks bigger than
other stars because it is
closer to us.

The sun and other stars
we see are very hot.

They are like great balls
of fire.

The sun is far away. And
the air around us saves
us from the heat of the
sun. The air keeps the
earth from getting as
hot as the moon.
The moon has no air.

Many stars are in the sky
   all day.
They are far away.
The sun is closer and its
   light is much brighter.

It is so bright we can not
see the other stars in
the daytime.
Part of the time the moon
is in the daytime sky, too.
Sometimes it is bright
enough to see during
the day.

The sun is a star, but we
do not see it at night.

At night it is on the other
side of the earth.
If you took a fast airplane
at night to the other
side of the earth, you
would see the sun.
It would be day there. It
would be night here.

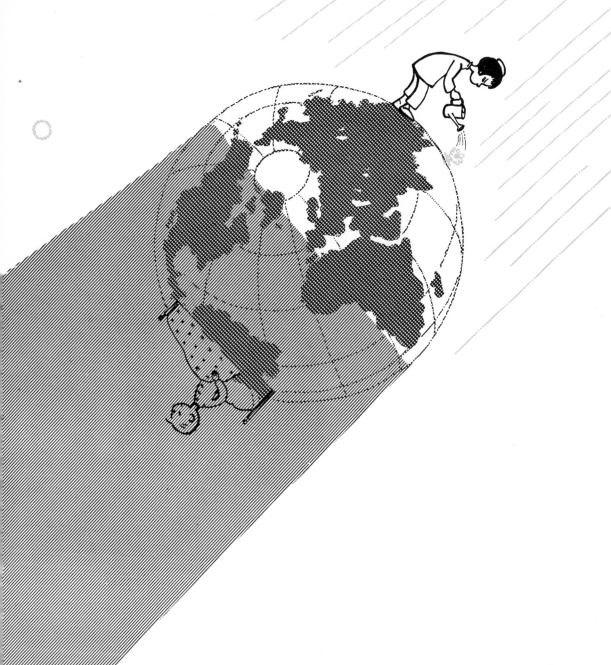

Did you see the sun set
last night? The sun does
not move when it sets.
We are the ones that
move.
As we turn, it looks as if
the sun were setting.
When the earth turns far
enough, we can not see
the sun.
Then we say it is night.

33

The moon turns around
   once in about four
   weeks.
The earth turns all the
   way around once in
   one day and one night.
You turn with the earth,
   but you do not fall off.

If you were here when you
had your breakfast...

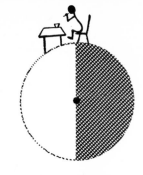

VIEW
FROM
SPACE
ABOVE
NORTH
POLE

you would be here when
you have your lunch...

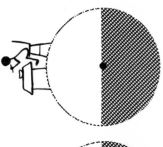

here at bedtime...

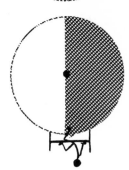

here in the middle of
the night...

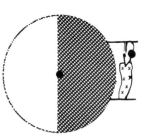

and back here for breakfast
the next morning.

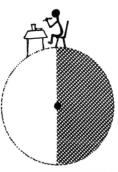

The earth holds you to it.

You do not feel upside
 down.

"Down" points to the
 middle of the earth.
 Your feet point "down."

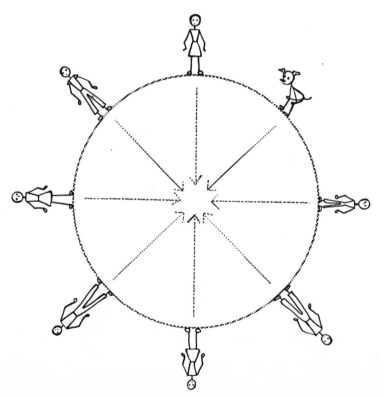

You do not feel yourself
move as the earth turns.
That is because the air
and everything around
you turns with you.
You move very, very fast.
The earth turns as fast as
most jet airplanes fly.

The earth goes even faster
in another way. It moves
around the sun. We
take the moon with us.
It takes our earth one year
to go around the sun.
Because it goes around
the sun, the earth is
called a "planet."
There are eight other
planets that go around
the sun, too. We are
like one big family in
the sky.

MERCURY

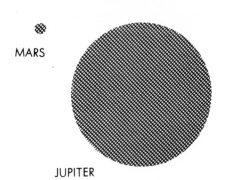

VENUS

EARTH

MARS

JUPITER

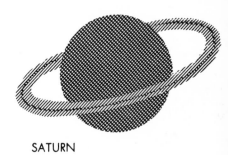

SATURN

URANUS

NEPTUNE

PLUTO

We know more about the earth than any other planet.

The other planets shine with the sun's light, just as the earth and the moon do.

Planets look like stars in the sky. But stars twinkle. Planets do not.

Two planets, Venus and Mars, sometimes can be seen in the daytime.

41

Planets and stars are
round like giant balls.
They do not have points
on them. The air makes
them look that way.

A "shooting star"
is not a real star.
It is a bit of rock
or stardust falling
through space. It
burns bright with
the heat it makes

as it passes through
the air around the
earth.

The sun gives us light and warmth. It makes plants grow and makes leaves green. It draws up water into clouds so it can rain.

The moon lights the earth at night.

Planets and stars help ships and airplanes find their way at night.

All are wonderful to see!